D1259151

INSPIRATION
for LIVING

Paul S. McElroy

Illustrations by

Chrystal Corcos

The Peter Pauper Press

Mount Vernon, New York

Inspiration for Living

Inspiration for Living

THE human mind cannot comprehend the greatness of God. A universe so vast that myriad galaxies stretch out into ever-expanding, unending space, an earth so minute that molecules are filled with invisible atoms separated from one another in space proportionately as great as the stars above, — this is a universe so complex that it is impossible for one to comprehend its greatness, much less the greatness of the Creator.

A GOD that is within man's capacity to understand, a god that is limited, is not a god at all. By very definition God is omnipotent and ominiscient and moves in mysterious ways His wonders to perform.

THE wise person will be thankful for such things as hardships through which he is made strong, for costly mistakes through which he learns to do better, for sickness through which he comes to realize his dependence upon others, for solitude through which he has time to think through his sense of values and the purpose of life, and for the struggles with the mystery and the unknown through which new joy is discovered.

THE love of money is the root of all evil, but the possession of it is an opportunity for much good.

IT does not pay to criticize or find fault.

No matter what minority interests we may represent, we are, as are others, at the same time members of a larger society whose more inclusive loyalties must be preserved. The part is never greater than the whole.

THE tragedy of life lies not in the fact that people must face trials and tribulations, nor in the fact that there are those situations which impose seemingly unfair hardships on innocent victims. The tragedy is that so many people are overcome by them. The tragedy is not that adversity comes, but that it is not endured. Religion should enable one to endure absolutely anything life may impose upon one.

THERE is no limit to the good a person can do, if he does not care who gets the credit.

LIFE is still rich in things to which one can give oneself, — social causes to serve, truth to be discovered, beauty to be created, friendship to claim one's loyalty. All of the great secrets of the world have not yet been discovered. Whether it be a frozen continent, a cosmic ray, or a lost coin, men have been driven to look for that which is hidden. There is no limit to what is "lost behind the Ranges. Lost and waiting for you, go!"

TRAVELLERS up the Nile marvel at the skill with which the Sudanese pilots navigate the steamboats in and out among the countless, shifting shoals of that treacherously shallow river. Seldom do these boats run aground. After watching one of these pilots maneuver the steamer up that river for several days, I was still puzzled as to how he could avoid the shoals so consistently, and in broken Arabic asked him how he did it. "Oh," said he, "I do not know where all the shoals are. After nineteen years of navigating I have come to learn only now where the deep channel lies."

৯

AN uncommitted person is a person without direction in life. He is like a ship without a rudder, and plenty of power but no direction.

৯

THE strongest things in the world often seem the weakest. For instance: Gentleness is stronger than cruelty, patience is stronger than impatience, mercy is stronger than revenge, and love is stronger than hate.

THAT there is a direct relationship between religion and good behavior, no one would deny. It usually follows that the genuinely religious person is also a person of good behavior, although it does not always follow that the person of so-called good behavior is also a deeply religious person. Religion is something more than good behavior. Religion is a point of view. It is not a way of looking at certain things, but a certain way of looking at all things.

୫ঌ

To whom much is given, much is expected.

୫ঌ

IF you criticize another person's efforts, just be certain that you can do the job better. Second, be certain that you would give of your time to do the job.

୫ঌ

THE reason why people fail is that they don't pray. They try to do by themselves what no man can do unless God be with him.

THERE is so much that needs to be done that opportunities for service are unlimited. Service is doing something without expectation or reward; it is doing something that does not have to be done, and possibly will not be done, unless you do it.

SUCCESS should be measured not so much by the position one has reached in life as by the obstacles which one has overcome while trying to succeed.

ON the way toward the great and noble goal toward which you strive you may befriend another and thereby fail to attain your own objective, yet in so doing you may achieve something which, in God's sight, is far more important. You may have enabled another to benefit mankind more than would be done in the achievement of your own goal.

WE become like what we love.

WE know so little, and we are so devoted to what little we think we know, and we see so many things only from our own viewpoint, that we should not expect the world, or even our little sphere of influence, to be run as we alone think it ought to be.

❧

DIFFICULTIES, rather than ease, extract the best that is in one.

❧

HAPPINESS consists not in having many things, but in needing few.

❧

THE concept of only one God for all the universe was at first such a revolutionary idea that centuries passed before it was generally accepted. That fact is not just an academic issue, but something that affects the life of every one. If there is only one God, then all people are brothers, children of the one Heavenly Father, and they are obliged to live with their fellowmen as brothers.

JUST as the mind is regarded as the seat of knowledge, so the heart is considered the seat of love. Our minds can help us make wise decisions on the basis of facts and information, but our hearts determine which way we will move in the light of that knowledge. People are seldom moved to action until the heart is affected. Undisciplined persons are often carried away by their emotions, and are not governed by their better judgment. That is why it is well to be committed to the highest — to love God with all your heart and mind and soul.

THE only thing in the world worth living for is to discover the will of God and do it.

THERE is no limitation to forgiveness; no injury so gross that it ought not be forgiven.

THE difficulty is that our concept of God is too small. God is infinite — infinite in his wisdom, goodness and love.

THERE are those who believe that all that is needed is to alter the attitudes and ambitions of individuals, and the redemption of the world will follow as a matter of course. There are others who believe that if the social and economic structure of society is altered, the redemption of individuals will then follow. The solution is not as clear-cut as either of these advocates would believe. It is not a case of either — or, of redemption either through the individual or through the social order. There is an interrelationship between the individual and society which must not be overlooked. The world needs people whose love is great enough to break through barriers. Social reconstruction will come when those in power have sufficient love in their hearts to forgive those under them.

❧

ECIDUJERP spelled backwards is prejudice; either way it does not make sense.

❧

A PERSON needs to be loved the most when he deserves to be loved the least.

14

How one responds to a situation may be of little consequence to the issue at stake. One decision may seem of little importance, but each decision helps to build character which is the sum total of decisions which one makes for oneself. Collectively, the decisions of many people will determine the strength of world forces that will be set in motion.

GENIUS is infinite patience.

IN all vicissitudes of life it is possible to be master of oneself. No matter how disturbed one may be, the important thing is to retain self-control in the face of adversity.

THE person of godly spirit does not measure success in terms of whether his feeble strength and skill are a fair match for the opposing forces. He measures success in terms of whether or not he does his part in what ought to be done.

THE potter pulls the clay for the handle of a pitcher from every possible side. With people, as with clay, outside pressure, properly absorbed, creates inner strength.

ह्र

To the extent that you influence history, you are an instrument of destiny.

ह्र

NEVER accept the negative until you have thoroughly explored the positive.

ह्र

INDIVIDUAL efforts may seem feeble and even futile, but one should not underestimate the extent of his influence for good or evil. One can never tell just what the result of one's actions will be; for with every deed he is sowing a seed, though its harvest he may not see.

ह्र

A RELIGION that does nothing, that gives nothing, that costs nothing, that suffers nothing, — is worth nothing.

THERE is joy in being committed to something greater than oneself. It is good to be gripped by higher loyalties. The secret of an integrated life is to choose a cause that commands the best that is in one, — something that one believes in with all one's heart, — and then to give onself to that cause with all one's mind and strength.

ૈ৯

"MY life may touch a dozen lives
    Before this day is done;
Leave countless marks for good or ill,
    Ere sets the evening sun."

ૈ৯

No person can be strong and pure and good without the world being better for it. Somebody will be helped or comforted by the very existence of that goodness.

ૈ৯

ONE of the best ways to appreciate the greatness of a person is to accept mercy and forgiveness from him.

18

THERE is a limit to the height or the distance that a person can throw a ball — beyond that maximum man has no control. The limits prescribed by nature represent determinism, but the way man controls the ball within those limits is free will. Determinism and free will are both part of life, but it is better to make the most of what is within one's control than to bemoan the fact that one cannot go beyond certain limits.

"THANK God for life!
E'en though it bring much bitterness and
        strife,
    And all our fairest hopes be wrecked and
        lost,
E'en though there be more ill than good in
        life,
    We cling to life and reckon not the cost.
    Thank God for life!"

YOU are bound to be tempted, again and again, but temptation can only become a sin when you fail to resist it.

EVERY effort on our part, however feeble it may seem, helps or hinders progress by just so much. One word, one deed, one minute, or one decision may seem inconsequential, yet every one of them counts.

SOMETIMES we have our hearts set on the wrong things, and what we regard as misfortunes or disappointments may be the very means of making possible what could otherwise not be achieved.

WHEREVER there is forward movement, there is bound to be turbulence.

ONE may be only a pawn or a victim of circumstances in the course of world events. But if one has to give up a career or perhaps sacrifice his very life, then it is still better to devote that life to being the best kind of person one can; thus one throws such strength as one has into the things one believes and into that which uplifts.

20

AT FIRST, even one minute spent in unaccustomed prayer will seem as endless as an empty silence or a blank stillness; but these periods of quiet can be lengthened profitably, and these times of silent stillness can become alive, eventually becoming the most rewarding experiences of the day, as one discovers how much God has to say to those who will listen. "In quietness and in confidence shall be your strength."

෫෯

IT IS noteworthy that the so-called seven deadly sins — pride, covetousness, lust, envy, anger, gluttony, and sloth — are all matters of attitude, inner spirit, and motives.

෫෯

DEVOTIONAL periods are often so crowded with our own thoughts that we spend our times of meditation talking to God and failing to allow Him to talk to us.

෫෯

LOVE is the most powerful force in the world.

GOOD intentions are essential, but in themselves they are not powerful enough to make you the kind of person you ought to be. The intent to be good and kind, honest, generous and forbearing are the fruits of an inner strength. The power to exhibit these virtues, these fruits, comes from the nature of the tree or of the person. There is only one way to insure good fruit and that is to make the tree good.

ᎦᏍ

ALL that which pleases is but for a moment. That only is important which is eternal.

Over great doors of Milan Cathedral

ᎦᏍ

To be one of thousands who have worked together to make possible some worthy event in history — that is our opportunity!

ᎦᏍ

IT is not our business to set the world right, but it *is* our business to do what we can within the little sphere of our influence.

SOME two thousand years ago, the Roman philosopher and statesman, Cicero, set forth six common fallacies which still obtain:

1. The delusion that personal gain is made by crushing others.

2. The tendency to worry about things that cannot be changed or corrected.

3. Insisting that a thing is impossible because we cannot accomplish it.

4. Refusing to set aside trivial preferences.

5. Neglecting development and refinement of the mind, and not acquiring the habit of reading and study.

6. Attempting to compel others to believe and live as we do.

IN the face of great danger or cruel opposition, the truly religious person will say, "I may lose my life in the struggle that lies ahead, but I would rather lose my life fighting for a cause in which I believe, than in dying for a cause in which I do not believe."

RELIGION places certain obligations upon one. A sincerely religious person cannot do certain things that others may do. For instance, he cannot advance himself at the expense of others; he will not speak unkindly about others; he cannot take all that he wants for himself when others must go without. It is also true that those who seek to make religion a vital force in life must do certain things that others may not do, such as going the second mile, acting justly, loving mercy, and walking humbly with God.

৪৯

THE great issues are decided either by the proponents or the opponents, never by the neutralists. The neutralists lose by default. Better it is to support one side or the other, than to do nothing and let another decide the issue for you, — perhaps in a way you disapprove.

৪৯

AROUND every person is a sphere of influence beyond which he cannot pass; but within range of that circle he is powerful and free.

YOU can spend so much time fretting about the past and things that cannot be changed, and worrying about the future and things which may never happen, that you lose the joy and fullness of the now, the present.

ॐ

THE danger of power lies in the fact that those who are vested with it tend to make its preservation their first concern. This means that they will naturally oppose any changes in the forces that have given them this power. Such people are reluctant to relinquish privileges voluntarily; that is why they have to be wrested from them forcibly, when need requires.

Victor de Wool

ॐ

PROBABLY the greatest need of the world today is for reconciliation. In order to establish a good relationship with others one must first admit his full share of responsibility; and if one has been wronged then he must be willing to forgive unconditionally — for partial forgiveness is not forgiveness at all.

LIFE brings enough difficulties without borrowing any from the future. Live each day at a time and with the assurance that God can be depended upon to carry you through any of tomorrow's troubles as surely as He has carried you through the troubles of the past.

MAY the great Spirit
Send his choicest gifts to you,
   May the Sun Father and the
Moon Mother shed their
   Softest beams on you,
May the Four Winds of heaven
   Blow gently on you,
And on those who share
   Your heart and wigwam.

Ojibway Chief's Prayer

A PERSON may be forced into doing things not to his liking and not of his choosing, but that does not prevent him from travelling along the path to a better self. He can still exert a positive influence for good.

27

WHEN men in a ship pull on a rope fastened to an anchor, they do not pull the anchor toward them but themselves toward the anchor. In the same way, when we pray, our words are not to pull God toward us but to pull us toward Him.

Clement of Alexandria

ॐ

IF you constantly compare yourself with others, you may become either unhappy or boastfully proud, for there will always be people greater or lesser than you. Remember that your mediocre gifts may contribute more towards the success of some project than the extraordinary talents of another. Believe in the worthiness of what you can do and be content in doing the best you can.

ॐ

THAT which you are able to do may seem small compared with what others accomplish, or compared with what you would like to do — but your little, if done well, may count for more than some more ambitious task, poorly done.

THE benefits of prayer are well-known, but the way to pray is less known. Effective prayer involves these six things:

A deep yearning to know God.

A willingness to trust God all the way and accept His answer.

A selflessness so complete that what happens to you is secondary.

A love or genuine concern for others and for God.

An ability to relinquish your hold so that you are not obstructing God's will.

The secret of prayer is to let go and let God.

ABSOLUTES change.

THE important thing is not what happens to one, but how one reacts to what happens. The tragedy is not that one must face ingratitude, injustice or adversity, but that one should let these conditions overcome him.

TRUTH is never wrong, but the purpose or motive for telling the truth needs to be considered. Is the purpose of telling the truth to hurt or to help another? It makes a difference how the truth is told, for words, even though truthful, can bring such offense that the damage done may offset the intended good. Therefore one should "speak the truth in love."

❧

WITHIN the span of our lifetime, we the living, and others of our generation, hold in our hands all that is of value from the past, and in those same hands we hold the hope of all that is to come. We are the living link, poised, if but for the brief span of a lifetime, in eternity, and through us will be transmitted the values of the ageless past to the timeless future.

❧

IF boiling water is poured into an empty glass it will crack, and if ice-cold water is poured into it, it will also crack; but if hot and cold water are mixed together before pouring, the glass will not crack.

IT IS the disciplined person who has the greatest freedom. The musician, for example, who through laborious hours of practice has mastered the instrument has much more freedom on the keyboard than the undisciplined or untrained individual. In the realm of character it is likewise the person who has mastered himself through discipline who finds more rather than less freedom in the decisions he must make.

ॐ

IF man learns, in time,
   To live in harmony
With all the things on Earth
   And his own human kind. . . .
He, too, like the turtle and the 'possum,
   May persist and live a million years.

Exhibit at Old Court House, St. Louis

ॐ

THE idealist believes that righteousness will ultimately triumph, and he voluntarily will throw his strength, such as it is, on the side of moral right rather than on the side of expediency.

MISFORTUNE may cause a set-back, but it need not mean defeat. It is not what happens to a person, but how he re-acts that is important. What seems a handicap may prove to be an asset or an opportunity.

CHARACTER is the sum total of decisions one makes for oneself.

THE process by which we can transform evil into good is by means of vicarious suffering. If evil is going to be transmuted into good, then it must be done by someone doing something at his own expense which will benefit another and promote the sum total of goodness in the world.

IT IS one thing to have more to do than you can get done in one day, but it is quite a different thing, and inexcusable, to neglect doing those things you could or should do each day.

To assume in time of misfortune that whatever has happened is for the best is but false comfort. It is not even true! Everything does *not* work together for good, nor does everything come out all right in the end. Only if the love for God is great enough to prompt you to put God's will above your own, then and then only, will you find that all events, even tragedies, will somehow work together for good — perhaps not your good, but for the good of God's kingdom.

A PERSON who does not understand another's silences will not understand his words either.

THERE comes a point beyond which you may have no control. Do all that can be done to achieve the desired results, and after having done all, then do not worry. Worry will not change the outcome.

THE smallest effort is not lost.

WHEN you are offended you have a choice of several reactions. You can ignore the situation and leave conditions unchanged; you can move away and avoid repetition through escape; you can retaliate and lower your standards to the level of the wrong-doer; or you can forgive and in that way try to heal strained or broken relationships. But in order to do this, you must be prepared to forgive frequently enough for your love and goodness to win their way into the heart of the one who has wronged you.

PROMOTION is two-thirds motion.

WHAT one thinks affects what he is, and what he is affects what he does.

WHAT you do, what you say, what you are, may help others in ways you never know. Your influence, like your shadow, extends where you may never be.

THANK God every morning when you get up that you have something to do which must be done, whether you like it or not. Being forced to work, and forced to do your best, will breed in you temperance, self-control, diligence, strength of will, content, and a hundred other virtues which the ungrateful will never know.

Charles Kingsley

ॐ

SUCCESS depends more upon zeal than ability, more upon mental attitude than on mental capacity.

ॐ

UNDERTAKINGS entered into half-heartedly often lack the extra or the plus that can lift them over the hurdle. Enthusiasm may mark the difference between success and failure.

ॐ

EVERY one is responsible for what takes place within the sphere of his control, and for no more.

WE receive so much that all we can give in return is but a pittance compared to the great needs that are all about us. When we take measure of our resources, we never find them depleted. We always have on hand more than we need. We should not be afraid of giving away too much because God's gifts to us have value only insofar as they are used.

৯৯

EVERY second is of infinite value.

৯৯

Do all the good you can,
By all the means you can,
In all the ways you can,
In all the places you can,
At all the times you can,
To all the people you can,
As long as ever you can.

Wesley

৯৯

WHAT is often asked of God is not so much His will and way, as His approval of our way.

ONE has no right to say of any good work that it is too hard to do; or of any misfortune that it is too hard to bear; or of any sinful habit that it is too hard to overcome. To do so is to admit defeat, and to lose by default. Help is always available.

ॐ

GOSSIP boomerangs.

ॐ

THERE isn't in all the world a perfect any-thing. The greatest picture has not yet been painted; the greatest play or poem or song has not yet been written; the best radio, or airplane, or church has not yet been built. Everything in the world remains to be done over or done better.

ॐ

GOD does not grant half a pardon.

ॐ

PERFECT obedience would bring perfect hap-piness, if only we had perfect confidence in the power we were obeying.

Hanna Smith

THE surest way to all happiness and perfection is to make it a rule to thank and praise God for everything that happens. For it is certain that whatever seeming calamity happens to you, if one thanks God for it, it can be turned into a blessing.

৪৯

"THIS I learned from the shadow of a tree,
That to and fro did sway upon a wall;
My shadow self, my influence, may fall
Where I may never be."

৪৯

YOUR answer to each decision may be based on a positive or a negative approach. You may envision its possibilities for good, or you may see in it only dangers and risk. You have, however, as much basis for building on your faith as on your doubt. Your very belief in a possibility may be the turning point between success and failure. Why not accentuate the positive?

৪৯

INTEGRITY is a requisite of greatness.

THE secret of happiness is to learn to live within one's limitations, whether they are physical, financial or circumstantial.

ৈষ

On earth you have a work to do before
Your life is done. That work may be a task
Concrete and seen with ease by those who
 ask
What you have done to justify your score.

Your work, perchance, may seem to be no
 more
Than helping some nonentity in need,
And yet to God a kindly word or deed,
Unsung, may be your part and count for
 more.

By earthly standards you may well succeed
And gain the praise of fellowmen sincere,
But if true gain you here would seek, you need
Forever towards God's standards persevere.

Success is measured not by worldly fame
But by the deeds of love done in God's name.

RELIGION teaches that you can be strongest where you are weakest. Just as in welding or in the fusion of metals, the weakest becomes the strongest, so when you conquer or absorb a weakness, the strength that lies in conquering that weakness passes into you and makes you stronger than before.

"THERE'S nothing so bad that it couldn't be
  worse;
There's little that time will not mend,
And troubles, no matter how quickly they
  come,
Eventually will come to an end."

WHETHER you have little ability or great ability and excel in many things, whether you have one talent or ten talents, is not of the greatest importance. What you do with what you have is what counts!

PERSEVERANCE makes many things possible.

THE success of a team depends upon how well the members play together and this means being willing to lose one's identity for the sake of the team.

ॐ

MAY YOU HAVE THE GRACE TO ASK GOD:

To give you judgment to see the right, courage to choose the right, and willingness to follow the right;

To build on faith rather than on doubts;

To move forward in the hope of what can be accomplished and not be held back by what cannot be done;

To see the possibilities in the new and not be paralyzed by the difficulties to be overcome;

To discover a sense of mission that life may be important and purposeful for you rather than dull and purposeless;

To measure values in terms of service to others rather than benefit to self.

ॐ

ASK always, "Is there a better way?"

THERE are six things the Lord hates; yea, seven are an abomination to him:

A proud look,

A lying tongue,

Hands that shed innocent blood,

A heart that devises wicked imagination,

Feet that are swift in running to mischief,

A false witness that speaks lies,

And he that sows discord among brethren.

Proverbs 6:16-19

છે

THERE are divisions in our community relationships which disturb and separate us, but the things which unite are actually greater than the things which divide us.

છે

BY procrastination one duty treads upon the toes of another, and then all duty seems irksome. The consequence is that one has no time to do the things that ought to be done.

TODAY's burden can be endured. It is when tomorrow's burdens are added to the burdens of today that the weight is more than a man can bear.

"YOU can never tell when you do an act
Just what the result will be;
For with every deed you are sowing a seed,
Though its harvest you may not see."

TREAT people as if they were what they ought to be and you help them to become what they are capable of being.

Goethe

ON first thought it may seem an anachronism to expect blessings from adversity, but there is evidence that the blessings of adversity may be more fruitful than the benefits of prosperity.

YOUR tastes determine your destiny.

47

IN the soul of human beings at their best there is an unconquerable spirit.

⊰⊱

"FREEDOM from hate unconditionally;
Freedom from self-pity;
Freedom from the fear of doing something
    that would help someone else more than it
    does me; and
Freedom from the kind of pride that makes
    me feel I am better than my brothers."

Duke Ellington

⊰⊱

THERE are sounds that elude you unless you are intent on hearing them. Listen not only to the words of others, but listen to their feelings. Train yourself to hear what they are trying to say to you.

⊰⊱

"FOR every evil under the sun
There is a remedy, or there is none;
If there is, seek and find it,
But if not, then never mind it."

PEOPLE grow apart needlessly. Most troubles could be avoided if people would give a little, be a little less self-centered, and try a little more to help each other.

❦

HE is wise who gives what he cannot keep in order to gain what he cannot lose.

❦

A USEFUL way of looking at prayer is to view it as "thinking in God's presence", as though lifted to the level of God's thought insofar as this is possible.

❦

HOLD your temper and keep your patience under all circumstances, for when you yield to vengeance you destroy or retard reconciliation.

❦

MERELY by being the very kind of person you are, you are exerting a greater influence upon others than you know.

49

IT IS easy to find fault with others, but it is not easy to live so that others will not see faults in us. We tend to criticize our friends for doing things that we could do no better.

ॐ

How often we think it is important to seem to be right whether we are or not.

Roy Longstreet

ॐ

IF the voices of all men cried out warning you to go the other way, if the faces of all men were turned one way and you met them face to face, — you going the other way — what would you do?

ॐ

To insist on having your own way is to assume that your way is the right way.

ॐ

WHOM the gods would destroy they first make mad with power.

KNOW your limits and where you are, if you want to get where you are going.

Ancient Genoa

ह&

WHEN it is dark enough, you can see the stars.
CHARLES A. BEARD, *as told to a student in response to a query.*

ह&

EVERYTHING you do is of importance because much which needs to be done will be done only if you do it.

ह&

WHAT you do may not be noticed by those around you. Perhaps you can get by with inferior workmanship, but the world is advanced by workmen with pride in their work. What man may not see, the immortals will.

ह&

SOME of the best lessons are learned from mistakes and failures.

51

WE never know how heavy a burden another person may be carrying.

⁊❧

"EVERY tho't that you've ever had,
Its own little space has fill'd,
Ev'ry deed you have done, good or bad,
Is a stone in the temple you build."

⁊❧

THE mills of God grind slowly, but they grind exceedingly small.

⁊❧

NOTHING can stop the person with the right attitude from pursuing his goal.

⁊❧

IT IS not so much strength that is lacking as it is will.

⁊❧

OUR satisfactions in life will be in proportion to our contributions.

THE greatest single qualification for a great man or a great team, is a desire to reach the objective without interference anywhere.

ॐ

IF the whole world followed *you,* would it be a nobler world?

ॐ

THERE is nothing noble in being superior to some one else; true nobility lies in being superior to your previous self.

ॐ

THE limits of faith are the mental barriers or doubts of one's own making.

ॐ

YOU have greater strength than you know. Emergencies call forth these reserves but will-power can be used to tap these resources.

ॐ

ANYTHING that separates one from God is wrong and sinful.

THE important thing is not what happens to you but what happens through you.

෨

THE longer a person puts off doing something he should do, the more difficult it is to get started.

෨

IT does not take great men to do great things; it takes dedicated men. Ordinary men, sufficiently dedicated, can do extraordinary things.

෨

ALL the troubles in the world cannot ruin a man unless they invade his inner life.

෨

GROWING old becomes almost agreeable when you consider the alternative.

෨

ABILITY may enable one to get to the top, but it takes character to keep one there.

IT IS easy to find fault with others when they do not conform to our pattern, but there may be reasons beyond their control for their behavior which we neither know nor understand.

THE bee fertilizes the flower it robs.

IT IS not enough just to get by, or do the minimum required. It is the extra that wins the victory.

LOVE is an active power. To use love towards an enemy is not to yield to him weakly but to conquer him by a force superior to his own.

IT IS well to ask God to change you instead of changing your circumstances.

GOD answers prayer when it enables one to act as He desires.

LORD, help me to be master of myself that I may be a servant of others.

SUCCESS often depends upon being able to tell whether you are up against a hopeless situation or just a difficult one.

SUCCESS consists of doing what you can do well.

PROBABLY the greatest need of the world to-day is for reconciliation. In order to establish a right relationship with others one must first admit his full share of responsibility, and if you have been wronged then you must be willing to forgive unconditionally, for partial forgiveness is not forgiveness at all. To admit your share of the guilt may not restore the damage done, but it will reassure the other person that your motives are not malicious. Admission of guilt and forgiveness are the twin foci around which reconciliation revolves.

HAVE you come close to victory, but missed out by just a little? What a difference a little more time would make, a little more patience, a little more understanding, a little more tolerance, or a little more strength! It is equally tragic to discover how much better off you would also be with just a little less of some things — a little less pride, a little less selfishness, a little less arrogance. There is tragedy in missing by a narrow margin. As Browning put it:

"The little more, and how much it is,
The little less, and what worlds away."

Do you encounter situations in which you cannot tell whether you are up against a stone wall or whether you are temporarily thwarted? The difference between success and failure is not great. Success often depends upon being able to tell whether you are up against a hopeless situation or just a difficult one. Here is a prayer, attributed to Reinhold Niebuhr, that may help when you are up against it:

"God, give me the strength to accept with

serenity the things which cannot be changed; give me the courage to change things that can and should be changed; and give me the wisdom to distinguish one from the other."

⟨❦⟩

RELIGION says that God can use you even with your faults and failures. God's purpose is not to punish but to save man. Much as the oyster can from a piece of grit make a pearl of great price, so God can take man's evil and use it. If that were not true, what a hopeless world this would be! No one is without sin, but somehow God works through imperfect lives to fulfill His purpose.

⟨❦⟩

SHOULD you tell the truth at all times and under all circumstances? Truth is never wrong, but it should be handled delicately and the purpose or motive for telling the truth should be considered. Is the purpose to hurt or help another? It makes a difference *how* the truth is told; for words, even though truthful, can bring such offense that the damage done may counteract the intended good. Always "speak the truth in love."

SICKNESS often brings with it serious and costly adjustments, but there is consolation in the fact that sickness need not be all loss or negative. Someone has said:

"When sickness comes and bids you rest
    awhile
  In some calm pool, beside life's too swift
    dreams,
Why rail at Fate, and count yourself ill used?
  'Tis then one's soul awakes, weaves dream
    on dream."

> GOD, give us grace
> Each in his place
> To bear his lot
> And murmuring not,
> Endure and wait and labor.
> *Martin Luther*, 1483-1546

ST. AUGUSTINE gave sound advice when he said; "Love God, then do as you please." If you love God sufficiently to want to do what is pleasing in His sight, then you need never worry about your own conduct, because things which will not please God will not be pleasing to you.

ENTHUSIASM may mark the difference between success and failure. Undertakings entered into half-heartedly often lack the extra or the plus that can lift them over the hurdle. A whole heart comes with confidence and with belief in what you are doing. As St. Paul said, "Whatever you do, put your whole heart and soul into it, as into work done for God."

I SIGHED because the day was dark — and then
   I met a child who had no eyes,
I complained because the walk was long —
   until I met a man who had no legs.
I prayed for wealth beyond my need — and
   then I met a poor soul with no bread at all.
Oh, God, forgive me — for the world is mine.
Source Unknown

NOTHING IS FINAL